Let's Celebrate Freedom!

A NATION OF IMMIGRANTS

Lorijo Metz

PowerKiDS
press

New York

Dedicated to T-Metz, who motivated me to immigrate to Indiana

Published in 2014 by The Rosen Publishing Group, Inc.
29 East 21st Street, New York, NY 10010

First Edition

Editor: Amelie von Zumbusch
Book Design: Colleen Bialecki
Photo Research: Katie Stryker

Photo Credits: Cover DEA Picture Library/De Agostini Picture Library/Getty Images; p. 5 Matej Hudovernik/Shutterstock.com; p. 6 Stock Montage/Contributor/Archive Photos/Getty Images; p. 7 Buyenlarge/Contributor/Archive Photos/Getty Images; p. 8 MPI/Stringer/Archive Photos/Getty Images; p. 11 Hulton Archive/Staff/Getty Images; p. 14 Claver Carroll/Photo Library/Getty Images; p. 15 Universal Images Group/Contributor/Getty Images; p. 16 Vlad G/Shutterstock.com; p. 17 Lewis W. Hine/Stringer/Hulton Archive/Getty Images; p. 18 Justin Sullivan/Staff/Getty Images News/Getty Images; p. 19 Hulton Archive/Stringer/Archive Photos/Getty Images; p. 20 Allison Joyce/Stringer/Getty Images News/Getty Images; p. 21 Monica M. Davey/Stringer/AFP/Getty Images; p. 22 John Moore/Staff/Getty Images News/Getty Images.

Publisher's Cataloging Data

Metz, Lorijo.
A nation of immigrants / by Lorijo Metz. — First edition.
 p. cm. — (Let's celebrate freedom!)
Includes index.
ISBN 978-1-4777-2899-4 (library binding) — ISBN 978-1-4777-2988-5 (pbk.) —
ISBN 978-1-4777-3058-4 (6-pack)
1. Immigrants — United States — History — Juvenile literature. 2. United States — Emigration and immigration — History — Juvenile literature. I. Metz, Lorijo. II. Title.
JV6450.M48 2014
304.8—d23

Manufactured in the United States of America

CPSIA Compliance Information: Batch # W14PK4: For Further Information contact Rosen Publishing, New York, New York at 1-800-237-9932

CONTENTS

Have you ever heard the lines "Give me your tired, your poor, Your huddled masses yearning to breathe free"? These lines from Emma Lazarus's poem "The New Colossus" explain why many **immigrants** moved to the United States. A plaque bearing the poem even hangs inside the Statue of Liberty.

More so than any other country in the world, the United States owes its existence to immigrants. Between 1820 and 1930 alone, nearly 37 million immigrants moved to the United States. Some came because their own countries were no longer safe. Most arrived dreaming of new **opportunities** and freedom. New immigrants still arrive every day.

The Statue of Liberty stands in New York Harbor. In the past, it was the first thing that many immigrants saw as they entered the United States.

NATIVE AMERICANS

Thousands of years before immigrants began arriving, Native Americans were already living in North America. There were many Native American peoples, with different languages and **cultures**. When Europeans first arrived, Native Americans were glad to trade with them. In exchange for iron and horses, they taught the Europeans how to plant crops like corn and other skills needed to survive.

This picture shows one of the Lenape villages that existed on Manhattan Island before European settlers arrived. The Lenape are also known as the Lenni Lenape and the Delaware.

This 1875 photograph shows several members of the Sioux people. The Sioux lived in the Upper Midwest. They were forced onto reservations in the late nineteenth century.

However, as more Europeans immigrated to America, they began driving Native Americans off their lands. In 1830, the United States passed the Indian Removal Act. This law eventually forced most Native Americans onto **reservations**, or land set aside by the US government.

In 1565, Spanish settlers established St. Augustine in Florida. It was the first permanent European settlement in what is now the United States. Several European countries established **colonies**, or lands they ruled, in North America. People from these countries came and settled the land.

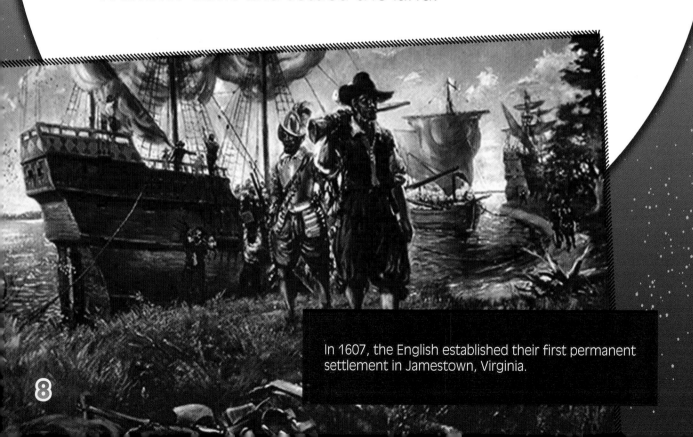

In 1607, the English established their first permanent settlement in Jamestown, Virginia.

EUROPEAN CLAIMS IN NORTH AMERICA IN 1750

KEY

- French claims
- British claims
- Spanish claims
- Russian claims
- Unclaimed land

These people came for many reasons. Many were farmers who could no longer make a living in their home country. Land was easier to buy in America than in Europe. Some, such as the English Puritans and Pilgrims, sought religious freedom. In 1776, settlers in 13 English colonies declared their independence from England. The colonies soon united to form the United States.

UNWILLING IMMIGRANTS

Not all early immigrants came freely. Hundreds of thousands of Africans arrived bound in chains. Sold as slaves to whites, they lived in poor conditions and worked long hours with little hope of freedom. White owners tried to get slaves to forget African culture. However, slaves did remember African music, stories, and **traditions**, and these became part of American culture.

In 1808, the United States banned bringing new slaves from Africa. However, people who were already slaves remained so. Over time, northern states outlawed slavery. However, most slaves did not gain their freedom until the end of the Civil War, in 1865.

In 1619, a Dutch ship arrived in Jamestown, Virginia. The 20 captured Africans on board became British North America's first slaves. Unlike later slaves, these Africans were probably not slaves for life.

TIMELINE

September 8, 1565

The Spanish establish St. Augustine, Florida.

August 20, 1619

African slaves arrive in Jamestown, Virginia. The American slave trade begins.

1550   1575   1600   1625   1650   1675   1700   1725   1750

May 14, 1607

The British establish a settlement in Jamestown, Virginia.

February 2, 1848

The Mexican-American War ends. Many Mexicans living on lands won by the United States become US citizens.

January 1, 1892

Ellis Island Immigration Station opens in New York Harbor.

1775   1800   1825   1850   1875   1900   1925   1950   1975

May 6, 1882

The Chinese Exclusion Act bans Chinese immigration to the United States.

October 3, 1965

The Immigration Act of 1965 is signed.

13

MEXICAN AMERICANS

Mexico, directly south of the United States, was another source of new Americans. From 1846 to 1848, the United States fought the Mexican-American War. Afterwards, Mexico turned the land that is now California, Nevada, Utah, Texas, most of New Mexico and Arizona, and parts of Colorado and Wyoming over to the United States. Many of the nearly 75,000 Mexicans living there chose to remain and become US citizens.

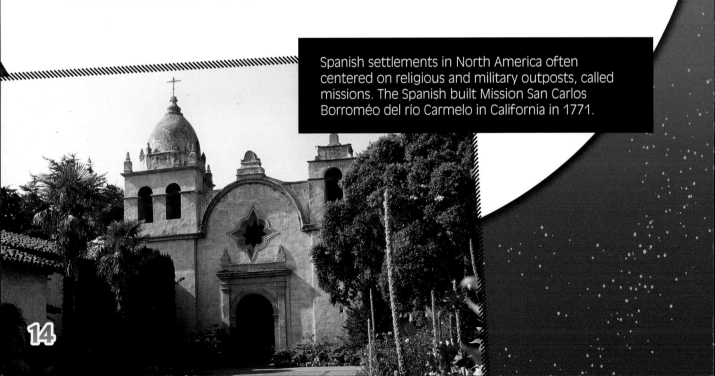

Spanish settlements in North America often centered on religious and military outposts, called missions. The Spanish built Mission San Carlos Borroméo del río Carmelo in California in 1771.

The Battle of Churubusco was part of the Mexican-American War. The war was fought between the United States, a former British colony, and Mexico, a former Spanish colony.

Between 1820 and 1930, nearly 750,000 Mexicans became Americans. Some were Mexican immigrants who moved north. In 1910, a **revolution** broke out in Mexico. Thousands of Mexicans fled to the United States, where they remained.

LOOKING FOR A BETTER LIFE

Between 1800 and the start of World War I, in 1914, nearly 25 million people immigrated to the United States. Most came from European countries, such as Germany, Ireland, and Italy. New immigrants often settled in **ethnic** neighborhoods, in which everyone came from the same country. These neighborhoods were often noisy and crowded. People living there were usually poor.

Between 1892 and 1954, about 12 million immigrants passed through the immigration station at Ellis Island in New York Harbor.

In the mid-nineteenth century, most immigrants came from northern and western Europe. After 1890, immigrants from eastern and southern Europe, like this Italian family, became most common.

Americans whose families had arrived earlier tended to look down on newer immigrants. In time, each wave of immigrants became accepted in American **society**. The immigrants' cultures made American culture richer, while the immigrants' children benefited from the opportunities America had to offer.

ASIAN IMMIGRANTS

Like other immigrants, Asians came for the opportunity for a better life. News of the California gold rush in 1849 brought many immigrants from China. Most found work digging in mines or building railroads. Beginning in the 1880s, immigrants came from Japan to work on Hawaii's sugarcane plantations.

Most Asian immigrants arrived in western states, such as California. Many came through the immigration station at Angel Island in California's San Francisco Bay.

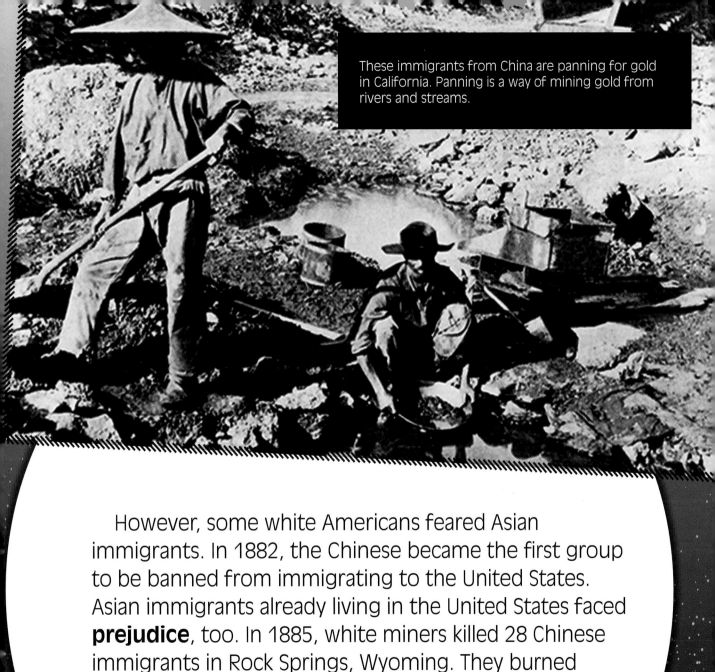

These immigrants from China are panning for gold in California. Panning is a way of mining gold from rivers and streams.

However, some white Americans feared Asian immigrants. In 1882, the Chinese became the first group to be banned from immigrating to the United States. Asian immigrants already living in the United States faced **prejudice**, too. In 1885, white miners killed 28 Chinese immigrants in Rock Springs, Wyoming. They burned Chinese homes and businesses, too.

By the early twentieth century, some Americans believed there were too many immigrants. The Immigration Act of 1924 banned almost all Asians from immigrating to the United States. When the **Great Depression** hit, in 1929, people feared that immigrants would take the few jobs available. The government even began sending Mexican immigrants back to Mexico.

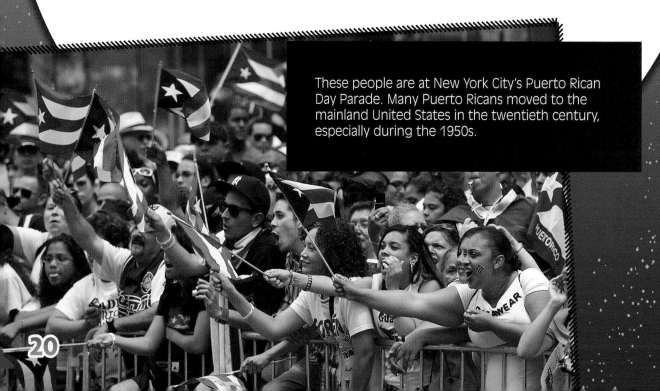

These people are at New York City's Puerto Rican Day Parade. Many Puerto Ricans moved to the mainland United States in the twentieth century, especially during the 1950s.

Early twentieth-century immigration laws kept out certain ethnic groups. The Immigration and Nationality Act of 1965 tried to correct this. It said that immigrants would be **admitted** because of their skills, rather than the countries from which they came. By the late twentieth century, Asia and Latin America were the biggest sources of immigrants.

India became a major source of immigrants in the later part of the twentieth century. Between 1970 and 2000, more than one million Indians moved to the United States.

21

IMMIGRANTS TODAY

Laws currently limit the number of immigrants allowed to enter the United States. Because of this, some immigrants arrive illegally. One such immigrant is Jose Antonio Vargas, a prize-winning journalist who was born in the Philippines but raised in the United States. Vargas is helping lead the fight to let **undocumented** immigrants who grew up in the United States become legal citizens.

The opportunities that the United States offers draw millions of immigrants here. In turn, immigrants make America a more interesting place to live!

Today it takes a lot of work to become a US citizen. Even so, thousands of people immigrate to the United States each year. These kids are immigrants from Tibet.

GLOSSARY

admitted (ed-MIT-ed) Allowed to enter.

colonies (KAH-luh-neez) New places where people move that are still ruled by the leaders of the countries from which they came.

cultures (KUL-churz) The beliefs, practices, and arts of groups of people.

ethnic (ETH-nik) Relating to a group of people who have the same race, nationality, beliefs, and ways of living.

Great Depression (GRAYT dih-PREH-shun) A period of American history during the late 1920s and early 1930s. Banks and businesses lost money and there were few jobs.

immigrants (IH-muh-grunts) People who move to a new country from another country.

opportunities (ah-per-TOO-nih-teez) Good chances.

prejudice (PREH-juh-dis) Disliking a group of people different from you.

reservations (reh-zer-VAY-shunz) Areas of land set aside by the government for Native Americans to live on.

revolution (reh-vuh-LOO-shun) A complete change in government.

society (suh-SY-eh-tee) A group of people who have something in common.

undocumented (un-DO-kyuh-men-ted) Not having the official paperwork that the law requires.

INDEX

WEBSITES

Due to the changing nature of Internet links, PowerKids Press has developed an online list of websites related to the subject of this book. This site is updated regularly. Please use this link to access the list: www.powerkidslinks.com/lcf/immig/